MW00907082

Lillie
Magida

A Conversations for Action and Listening
Publication

Javi's Opportunity Manual

A Kid's Guide to Making Things Happen

María Flores Letelier

J L Flores

Illustrations by Angela González

ISBN-978-0-9977110-2-8

Library of Congress Control Number: 2016916479

BISAC: Juvenile Fiction / Social Issues / Self-Esteem & Self-Reliance

Conversations for Action and Listening Publication

For Rodolfo.

Chapter 1
The Major Revelation

Today, I stumbled across what I believe to be a MAJOR revelation. Well, it's major for a kid, at least. I noticed that the loud kids —who make a lot of noise and insist until they get what they want— usually get their way. There's this one kid at school, Sebastian, who has this tactic down. About twice a week, when his parents come to pick him, Sebastian kicks and screams like a broken car alarm for about five minutes. The next day, with a big smile written all over his face, he's holding a new toy in his hands. Who would have thought?

My baby sister is a total pro at this strategy. Whenever she wants something, she first softly states what she wants. It's more of a soft murmur: "I wan i-cream." Then, when they say no, she cries at the top of her lungs: "I WANNNN IIIIIICREEEAM!"

Sometimes, the high-pitch, streaky noise even makes the next-door neighbor´s dog cry! Of course, no one wants problems with their neighbors. At least that's the excuse my parents always use for simply giving in to little Amalia.

But that's just not my style. I'm twelve now. Gotta respect THE age. The age itself calls for a step up the "maturity ladder". I mean, twelve is almost thirteen. And thirteen is teenage years. Now THAT is really big.

Besides, half the time, when I want something, I feel no different than a dog barking out loud with everyone around me going about their business. This is what happened with tennis camp recently. When I said that I wanted to go to tennis camp this summer my parents ignored me. It's time to come to terms and face the facts: something isn't working with my approach!

Watching Benji García, on the other hand, makes you think. Benji is a seventh-grader who wanted to make some money to hang out with his friends on weekends. His parents wouldn't give him all the money he needed for movies, snacks at the movies, and ice cream afterwards. Let's get one thing clear from the start: an afternoon out with friends can really cost ya.

But Benji doesn't resort to whining, kicking, or screaming like the kid Sebastian or my little sister do. Benji has a band at school, where he's the lead guitar player. He's pretty good, for a seventh-grader, that is. He's no Beethoven —you know, the genius musician with an angry face from hundreds of years ago— but genius ideas do come to Benji. The most genius of all the genius ideas I have EVER witnessed happened recently: Benji asked all the teachers to give flyers and send people his way for guitar lessons. And guess what? They actually did it! I was in awe when

12

I saw the teachers giving the flyers to the parents. And guess what? The parents actually booked him! He makes $5.00 for every thirty minutes he spends with aspiring rock-n-rollers. Unbelievable! He has the teachers working for him and parents paying him. Benji literally moved heaven and earth just to get to go to the movies! And he accomplished this great miracle without any DRAMA. A lot of my friends have become really dramatic lately. I am not sure why this is happening now at twelve years old. But not Benji. Benji clearly respects The Age. You can really learn from watching a kid like him.

I became more and more impressed as I watched even more teachers pass out flyers for Benji.

I have to ask: What do the Benji's of this world do right? Are they simply nicer, smoother, more charming than the rest of us? Benji's pretty nice, but I wouldn't call him smooth or good at smooth talkin' by any means. I've seen smooth.

Dimitry Skakakun. Now HE is smooth, smooth as the silky sheets my mom won't let us sit on, or at least he seems to think so. He always slows down his pace when he passes the *Comadres* -the girls clique that seems to be growing day by day- and somehow manages to lightly bump into one of them on the shoulder. Then he looks up and gives them that special "I know you like me" look, with a slight wink each time. The *Comadres* act irritated, but then, no matter how much they try to disguise it, I see little grins push their way out of their tightly closed lips.

So Dimitry has a way of getting things. It's much more roundabout than the way Benji goes about getting things. I just don't think that Dimitry's style is one that I could ever adopt. I mean, I can't even try to imitate THAT look.

Benji, on the other hand, goes about things in a much more direct manner. For instance, when he asked Mrs. Lee to hand out flyers, he literally asked for help: "Mrs.Lee, will you please pass out these flyers when parents come to see you?"

Benji has no issues with asking for help or asking for what he wants.

OK, I get it. Ask for what you want! That's what I'm always telling my friend Natsuki. Natsuki always wants people to read her mind.

"Natsuki, what do you want to play today? Do you want to play kickball? What about painting? Do you want to go to the park?"

She simply shrugs her shoulders with a blank stare on her face. Then it hit me: the game she wanted to play is: "Let's make Javi do a round of guessing games." Well, that is about as fun as watching the grass grow. Natsuki has a hard time stating what she wants. I think the adult term here is ASSERTING herself. She's like this even with simple decisions, like deciding whether she wants apple or orange juice, always answering "I dunno know."

If we stay silent, how will others ever know what we want? Although when my little sister Amalia cries, somehow *mami* knows that she wants her milk. *Mami* does read minds! But I think this strategy only works for babies and toddlers, and maybe a few small children. I can testify from first-hand experience, parents lose the magic skill of reading our minds as we get older. I think the cut-off age for parent mind-reading is

15

something like six years old. When you turn seven, forget about ever trying this tactic. There's no way of getting around it—we have to ask for what we want.

So why do I hang out with a silent sidekick? Despite having to put up with several rounds of tortuous guessing games, Natsuki has been my best friend since second grade now. She's the most loyal person I know. She is quirky. And I like quirky. Natsuki definitely skips to the beat of her own drum, something I admire in a person. Natsuki and I kind of wound up together since both of our parents didn't put us in Girl Scouts or ballet classes, or tennis camp. All of the other girls at school seemed to know each other from all those groups or classes. Natsuki's mother is big on her taking private piano classes, but that's about it. And piano is a one-person activity—it doesn't require any interaction with other kids. That's probably why Natsuki is somewhat quiet at school, which I don't mind since I talk so much. *Mami* says I was born talking.

Besides, Natsuki's the only friend who will put up with my odd ways. such as wearing bulky running shoes with skirts, or climbing trees. I'm not ready to give up my tomboy ways just yet. My other friends have increasingly joined the *Comadres* network. The *Comadres* are fine, it's just that once you join the group, you have to submit to the "anyone." I'm not a rebel or anything, I mean, I haven't pierced anything or dyed my hair green yet.

But I refuse to submit to the "anyone."

THE ANY ONE

Since I was little *mami* loved to read literature and philosophy to me at bedtime instead of the typical children's bedtime stories. She especially loved to read philosophers who talk about the "anyone". She taught me that the "anyone" is just what everyone does, what everyone is supposed to do—you're supposed to get good grades, you're supposed to wear certain name brands or fashion, you're suppose to do what everyone does, you get my line of thought? Some things the *Comadres* do, such as tennis camp, are fun—IF you like tennis. But doing things just because "one" is supposed to do them, well, I find myself increasingly developing an allergic reaction to THAT way of thinking. *Mami* says some of us Latino immigrants fall hard into the "anyone" trap. We try so hard to "move on up"

18

that we end up blending, losing some of our initial spunk that got us here in the first place. I mean, to leave one's comfortable country and start from scratch somewhere else takes serious "I don't give a hoot what others think of me" guts, you know?

Why suddenly do I feel the urge to do something that is different? Well, different for me at least.   Maybe my cousin Claudio will understand what I am going through.

Chapter 2
The Nation of Chimbalitza

From: javiera.vega2001@gmail.com

To : ClaudioMoraV@hotmail.com

Subject: Hello there

Primo! Or Cousin as we say here. How are ya doing over there in the other America? I know I should write you in Spanish, but *mami* tells me that *Tía* Angelica is on you about improving your English. I guess we're in the same boat—*Mami* gets on me as well about speaking more grammatically APPROPRIATE Spanish.

Do you remember when we came to this country? I was only four, what does she expect? Can you believe that, until fourth grade, I thought "enjoyarse" meant to "enjoy oneself" in Spanish because *mami* would always tell us that she was "enjoyando" this or that, enjoyando *abuela*'s food, enjoyando *vacaciones*. I took pride in my perfect Spanish. Until......

Don't get me wrong: up until now, I didn't mind having lived in three different countries. Not everyone gets to travel to two other countries to visit family members, well, at least to Latin America (I especially enjoyed visiting you guys). It's just that, you know, I'm starting to feel a little different from the other kids. You see, most kids here have been doing the same thing all of their lives, same neighborhood, same friends, same sports, and same clubs. Same EVERYTHING.

I wish you could see the *Comadres*.-the girls clique at my school. I mean, these girls were born here. So what if they call their aunts *Tías* or their grandmothers *abuela* like I do. This is all they know. They all grew up taking the same ballet classes and music classes, Girls Scouts, and whatever classes are "in." They even dress alike—they all wear skinny jeans and ballerina flats every day! Now they're becoming an even tighter group: they talk alike, smell alike, and I think they're even starting to breathe at the same pace!

The Comadres!

And they really don't care if I lived in other countries before coming here.

The whole scene makes me giggle. I mean, I always knew I was somewhat different—maybe a little taller than the rest......

I guess that's why people have always asked me where I'm from. I get asked that so much that sometimes I make up a country. Surprisingly, most people don't ask any more after that.

I shouldn't complain, really. I heard that you're studying your butt off over there for who knows what. Mom says jobs are tough there, especially for those that don't speak English.

So here it is. I can help you practice your English and you can listen to me vent. An OPPORTUNITY for both of us. (Though I think I'll be getting the better end of this deal.)

OPPORTUNITY. The magic word. The word I've been hearing my parents ramble on and on –or should I say, sing– about (you know how much our family loves to sing) since we arrived to this country. America is the land of opportunity. Opportunity is at our doorstep—so everyone says! This is the place where you can grow up without any money or powerful family ties and still be somebody. Just look at President Abraham Lincoln, and all the self-made folks in history. Look at Madonna— better yet, don't look too close (smiley face).

Now that I'm entering sixth grade, I've started to wonder more about how we get opportunities. You see, I'm set on a mission. This year, I'm set on going to tennis camp. All the kids at the school I go to get to go to some sort of summer camp. Until now, not me. Well, that's all about to change! When I mentioned to *Mami* and *Papi* that I wanted to go to tennis camp this summer, they simply ignored me.

Mami and *papi* say "just be grateful you get to go to that school at all." It sure doesn't feel great when I'm left all alone in the summer time, but I get the point. It's a nice school. The neighborhood is pretty great as well. I live about forty minutes outside of the city. You can actually see city lights from the hill at my nearby park, where kids from my neighborhood gather to play tennis, basketball, and to feed the ducks. The houses are built on tree-lined streets, mostly one-story, ranch-style houses with large yards for playing soccer, or "fútbol" as you say over there. The folks that come here do so for the school, even if it means a long commute for *papi* to work. *Mami* and *papi* have sacrificed a lot so that I can go to school here, as I am sure *Tía* Regina has told you. I know my parents work hard and are busy.

But it does get pretty lonely here in the summer when everyone is away at summer camp and I am stuck at home. Do you know what I really want? I really, really want to be like Serena William some day. So far I am self-taught. I taught myself tennis with an old racket my dad had in the garage, mostly by bouncing the ball against our backyard wall. I was able to get this boy from my neighborhood, Aaron Scott, to play with me a few times. At the tennis court, someone said I had REAL potential! That's right. REAL potential—I think that means not FAKE. Remember I told you that I had been doing gymnastics with the local volunteers at the "Y" since I was six? I finally reached "advanced level," and there were no more classes for girls my age or height. Since then, I've been antsy to do something, and to do it well.

This summer is going to be different. I'll make sure of that before these last couple of months of school end. I want to really get to play. Can you imagine me, a world champ one day? That would be a first for our *familia*. I have to go to camp, you see, to train with the real pro's.

I'm on a mission. Soaking it all up. Watching everybody and taking notes.

I hope I don't sound too spoiled or selfish with my American dreams. I really don't mind what *mami* and *papi* call "the important things"—helping out around the house, playing with my baby sister Amalia, hanging out with *abuela*. "Family first" *mami* always says. That's fine with me. I look forward to our *comida*s or meals together with my aunts, uncles, *abuelos*, and cousins every Sunday.

It's hard not to dream big here, everyone seems so active in my world. You should see how the kids at my school all play sports. Sports is not an option here—you do a sport or you do a sport. Everyone in my generation grew up with the "Just Do It" buzz. It's such a different world from where *mami* and *papi* came from.

Claudio, I know that getting an OPPORTUNITY is important for you and all of your folks in Latin America as well. I'm going to put together an OPPORTUNITY MANUAL! I am hoping to come up with some lessons that will help me understand this whole opportunity thing. Maybe I can do something selfish for me and self-less for you. I have ten weeks left to get the money for tennis camp. If I can learn some lessons each week, I'm hoping that by the end of week 9 I'll be ready to go to camp.

Alright cuz, I gotta run. I am going to start this journal once and for all. Talk to you again real soon!

Un *abrazo* or Hugs!

Javi

It's hard to focus on tennis camp when my best friend won't share this passion with me. Natsuki doesn't like tennis. She doesn't like sports, actually. Maybe I haven't been to Girl Scouts or camps of any sort, but in case I didn't mention it, I'm quite athletic, you see.

Ever since first grade, I could outrun my whole class in P.E. I even won primary grade champion in third grade for the school walk-a-thon. Some of the boys were mad that a girl won. They said I should have come in second, that a boy named Reeves really beat me by 0.01 mile or something. Unfortunately for Reeves, he never turned in his sponsorship money. The way I see it, I walked at least 2 miles, if not more, around my

neighborhood collecting my sponsorship money one household at a time. So that should more than make up for the 0.01 mile, right?

Any free chance I get to participate in a competition, whether it's during P.E. class, after school or racing competitions on my block, I'm in! *Mami* and *papi* and the rest of our family used to laugh at me, because for years I would wear socks and tennis shoes even in 95-degree weather, even when I was supposed to dress up for something.

30

I'm ready to do more than race the boys in my neighborhood up and down the block. Maybe I shouldn't say it out loud. My *abuela*, my grandmother, says that Latinos aren't supposed to appear as though we want to outshine anyone. We can do our best, but in the end, what will happen, will happen—the destiny factor. (My grandmother's favorite phrase is "*Si Dios quiere*"— God willing).

"Keep your long-term goals to yourself, you might jinx them if you say them out loud." After all, it's arrogant to presume one can plan too far ahead."

"Only God knows what is in the future."

But I'll say it anyway, after all. I really, really want to excel at something—to achieve excellence, not just be good enough at something. There, I said it. I'll need real classes this time around. I need serious training, like any aspiring athlete who wants to succeed. For now, it looks like I'm on my own. Natuski and my *mami* or *papi* don't seem to get it. Is it so strange to want to excel at something?

✮ ✮ ✮

I'll need to figure out this whole opportunity thing first. I can't excel at anything if I sit here waiting for opportunities to come to me, right? When I look at all the great folks who have made it in this country, out of nothing, I am certain that they went after opportunity. I am sure of it. There must be a way to grasp opportunity!

Papi tells me that I'm lucky, I have a chance at being a professional. Cousin Fabi is at the university studying to be a lawyer. *Papi* was able to validate his accounting license for

31

this country. But who I really admire is *Mami*, who recently transferred from the community college to the state college, where she's studying literature. Her friends tell her she should study nursing, something more PRACTICAL. *Mami* says literature teaches her to be more articulate, to write well, and to study different WAYS in which people live. *Mami's* way of looking at things is not common in our family.

Go to good schools, study hard, find a way to become a professional, and you'll achieve peace and happiness. Studying and getting good grades is fine, I just have an intuition that there's more to the story. I wonder whether being a professional is the same as achieving peace and happiness. Take my *papi*, for instance. He often walks around with a wrinkled frown written between his eyes, his face tight and tense, as if a hurricane of worries just hit him.

☆ ☆ ☆

But enough with the violins! Let's get back to the relevant task here: the lessons for my Opportunity Manual. What's really amazing about Benji is that he can do what most kids only dream of. He's able to get adults to work for him. The awesome thing is that people are happy to do it. They're happy to pass out flyers and they're happy to take his classes.

So what is Benji García doing? Tennis camp is one week closer, so let me start writing down lessons for my Opportunity Manual.

Screaming at
the top of your
LUNGS
only works for a
gifted FEW.
Try this strategy
at your own risk.

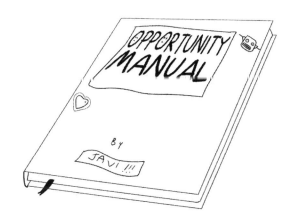

ASK for what you WANT
If you can find a way
to get others to HELP,
You're struck GOLD!!!

Chapter 3

Stepping up the Maturity Ladder

My *Tío* Bill, or Uncle Bill, came over for dinner this evening (we all call him *Tío* –which means "uncle" in Spanish– even though he's from Montana. He doesn't seem to mind). What great timing! This is just the break I needed to get some new lessons for my Opportunity Manual. I was starting to wonder if anyone was going to say anything that would help me out.

Most of the time, people talk and talk, but as *mami* always says, talk is cheap. *Mami* says only few folks have anything INTERESTING to say. Since I seem to be quite a chatterbox, I didn't really get what *mami* meant. Until recently. I've been paying close attention to everyone's conversations, and I'm really amazed by it all. I mean, I thought I was a talker, but man, can some people talk and talk about the smallest details!

After a while, it just sounds like I'm listening to nothing at all—just bla, bla, bla, bla.

Tío Bill is different—he's not the typical family relative who treats kids as if we were still five years old. To be honest, *Tío* Bill didn't treat me like a five-year-old even when I WAS five years old.

Tío Bill has usually treated me more like a friend than an uncle, which at times felt a little weird. Most of the time, I had no idea what he was talking about. Lately, *Tío* Bill has been sharing new things he's been learning about being an "entrepreneur." Entrepreneurs? I thought to myself. Aren't those folks who have a business? Now, these people must know something about making opportunity happen. This is just what the doctor ordered for Javi!

I heard *mami* telling Tio Bill that most Latinos divide up into two groups: those that want their own business, and those that want to become a "professional". I can see what she is saying. *Tío* Pablo has dreams of starting a construction business, and he's been doing contractor work for many years now. Apparently, times are tough with the whole economy thing everyone talks about, but *Tío* Pablo persists. Some members of my family don't get it. *Papi* has been pushing me towards the "professional" route for a while, so you know what side he is on. I don't see *papi* particularly enthused with his choice, though.

But there is something I don't get about what *mami* is saying here. *Tío* Bill is an example of someone who doesn't fit neatly into either of the boxes, right? He's a lawyer, so we could put him in the "professional" box. But the beauty of it all is that he doesn't have a boss! He has his own law practices. He says he has clients and that he wants to "expand his client base." So I guess I could also put him in the business-owner box. *Tío* Bill has always confused me, since he doesn't fit neatly into any box. He's always using lots of big words, like "target market"… mostly words I don't understand well. When I was younger, I wasn't even sure if he was speaking English half the time. I even imagined that he was some sort of undercover agent sent by extraterrestrials to spy on my family.

Tío Bill does have INTERESTING things to say. I see now why *mami* and *papi* give him all their attention when he comes over. This last time he came over, I even listened to him. Really I did. I paid attention with every last nickel in my pocket! *Tío* Bill described this course he took on "entrepreneurship." He described it as more than having and growing a business, but actually being an "entrepreneurial" person who goes after opportunity. That's the word, that elusive word I've wanted to learn more about. After all, I am writing an Opportunity Manual, right?

Tío Bill went even further. The course taught him that it's not just about going after opportunity, it's about making opportunity happen. How cool is that? I sat there, paralyzed with awe. I could really make opportunity happen? How?

"The most important part of making opportunity happen," reported *Tío* Bill in a serious tone, "is communication, especially if you're trying to make something happen. When we need help for something, we communicate with others."

Communication? Asking for help? These ideas made a clicking sound —clickity click!— in my head. Natsuki doesn't communicate and Benji does! It's true. Nothing happens on our own.

"The way we communicate makes all the difference in whether we make things happen or not. When you make a REQUEST (asking others for something)..." *Tío* Bill paused as he gazed at his glass of water, as if to make sure we took heed... "you need to take some responsibility over what you are asking for."

While he sounded confident of what he was saying, I could tell that he also wanted to be careful with how he communicated to us.

"Look, I don't want to sound like I'm preaching. It's just that my eyes opened up when I realized that, when I make requests, I don't always make these with care or responsibly. Sometimes, we all fall into simply informing, demanding, or asking for things indirectly. And then we wonder why things aren't going as we hoped! I understand now why my assistant doesn't always understand what I'm asking for. We assume others can read our minds".

So announcing to others what you want without really asking or by being indirect doesn't work? Well, my sister Amalia is very good at demanding things indirectly. Sometimes, my parents even applaud her feeble attempts at making requests! Again, I guess that's just one of those things that works for toddlers, not for a twelve-year-old (almost 13, remember?).

Benji made an appearance in my head again. I imagined how Benji makes requests. He does seem to have a way of making a request that stands out. He doesn't just announce or inform, as most of us do. That's probably why it's hard to understand what we kids are saying half the time!

A small light (more like a mini-flashlight) was starting to illuminate this idea of how to make opportunity happen. I began to see that that making a request has something to do with what words or phrases you use—some phrases are ACTION words and some are lazy, sleepy and even whiny. "Will you help me?" sounds like an action phrase. The phrase can take us from one place to another that we'd rather be. Now I think I'm starting to see why *mami* has always said I'm whining when I say things like: "I wish someone would do so and so." I guess we can say that this isn't an ACTION phrase—it's a lazy phrase! Finally, another lesson for my Opportunity Manual!

If you want to get HELP, make a REQUEST using ACTION phrases, not lazy whiny or demanding BULLY-LIKE phrases!

✯ ✯ ✯

Now I just needed a chance to speak with *Tío* Bill all on my own. After all, I don't want to raise any suspicions, right? When my parents left the room to get desert, I raced over to *Tío* Bill like a ninja on a secret mission.

"You know *Tío* Bill," as I prepared my case, "I thought I was communicating with *mami* and *papi*. I just don't think they understand what really matters to me."

"I told them I wanted to go tennis camp this year, because I never get to go." I couldn't help but sigh, as the whole tennis camp family war was starting to overwhelm me.

"I want to grasp the opportunity, but *mami* and *papi* won't let me go. *Tío* Bill, please tell me, what's the right way to make this request?"

With a raised brow, *Tío* Bill looked at me firmly. Finally, someone was listening to me. He tilted his body towards me, and I, of course, continued on and on until he spoke and turned off my Javi chatterbox.

"Javi, are you sure you made a request, or did you announce that you want to go to summer camp? Just take a look at the memos on your refrigerator!"

43

Maybe I had never really REQUESTED to go to tennis camp. When I told my parents I wanted to go, they dismissed me quickly.

"Maybe you need to stop announcing what you want, and ask your parents for a conversation. Why don't you try making a PROPER request and see what they say? I can sit with you."

I anxiously waited for my parents to enter the dining room.

"*Mami, Papi?*," I dared to say, "Will you send me to tennis camp this year?"

At that moment, my mom confessed the reality of our money situation.

"Javi," *mami* gently whispered, "it isn't that we don't want you to go tennis camp, it's just that we can't afford it. I'm going to school, only working part-time, and *papi's* salary is just enough to pay all the bills and rent for this house so we can live in this school district. Javi, I'm not sure you're aware of how much things cost, so let me be direct with you. Tennis is an expensive sport: tennis classes cost money, tennis clothing is expensive, the racket itself is expensive and must be replaced. You've never asked us to pay for such an expensive activity before, so we just weren't sure how to let you down."

At that moment, *Tío* Bill did in fact read my mind. Before I even gave my "it's the end of the world" look, he spoke.

"When we make requests, it's possible that you are told no. This happens to me all the time when I'm out trying to get new business for my law practices. At least now your parents have listened to you, they know what matters to you, and they take you seriously. Even when we're told no, there are other "conversational moves" you can make here".

44

"Now this is getting interesting," I thought to myself, as *Tío* Bill paused for a moment.

"You see, Javi, making a request to go to tennis camp opens up a CONVERSATION. The response you are given isn't always the end of the world. So relax. You want to make something happen? Then you're the one who has to figure out how to make it happen. What's important is to keep the conversation moving forward and continue inventing your opportunity."

He looked out the window for a moment, as a school bus with a dozen noisy kids passed by.

"Relax? Sounds easy, but what's my next move, *Tío* Bill?"

"Good job Javi, you're listening! There are other 'conversational moves' you can make. You can PROPOSE a way to get over the money hurdle, am I making myself clear?"

The mini-flashlight was glowing brighter.

The fact of the matter is that NO was never an obstacle for me when I was little. When I was eight, I wanted this beautiful Cocker Spaniel, but my parents wouldn't buy it. So I settled for the first mammal I could find: a RACOON! Even though she was a girl racoon, I called her "Billy." I always wanted a little brother.

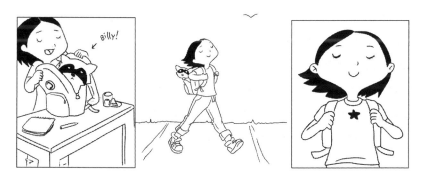

"I think I'm getting your point, *Tío* Bill. What if I propose raising funds for tennis camp?"

"Now you're getting the hang of conversational moves, Javi."

I felt myself step up the maturity ladder, and I jumped up as high as I could. Things are definitely changing. It was time to get to work!

CONVERSATIONS open up NEW paths for making opportunity happen. Being told "NO" is not the end of the WORLD! These are other conversational moves. But be CAREFUL with your choice of PETS!

Chapter 4

The Chatterbox

My first attempts at making what I thought were quite effective requests did not go over so well this afternoon. Since I have always been the chatterbox, I thought I was good at asking for things. Yet it felt like my requests were bouncing back at me just like the tennis ball does when I play tennis against my backyard wall.

Mami has her rules. Most of them make absolutely no sense to me. For instance, I can't sleep over at anyone's house until I turn thirteen, not even Natsuki's. Maybe this is because *mami* doesn't have time to do the whole "coffee" thing, where moms get together for morning coffee and talk about their kids. Maybe if she made time to get together with them, she would know them better, and let me stay over at their house.

What was happening? After all, spending the night at someone's house isn't expensive. Unless I'm mistaken, I won't be charged a bathroom fee or anything—spending the night at a friend's house is supposed to be free. Was I not communicating my request clearly? I thought I was quite charming, looking *mami* right in the eyes.

But that wasn't the worse of my communication fumbles with *mami*. Earlier this week, I got myself into an even bigger mess with what I now know was a badly made request. One night, I didn't have any pencils for doing my math homework. I was very upset. *Mami* wouldn't go out and buy pencils for me that night. She said that I never told her when I needed to have the pencils by, or what kind of pencils I needed. As you can guess, I didn't get my pencils on time. That did not go over so well at school.

So apparently I need to get better at this whole request thing.
But, man oh man, do old habits die hard! It was time to talk to
Tío Bill again.

"We all know how to demand what we want," Tío Bill
exclaimed with an "obviously Javi" tone of voice, "but making
'effecive requests' is entirely different. Javi, do you know what
'effective' means?"

Sure, I know how to look up a word in the dictionary:
Effective
(Del lat. effectivus).
1. adj. Accomplishing a purpose.
2. adj. Producing the intended effect.

Yet I had a feeling that this wasn't quite what Tío Bill was
trying to show me.

"Javi, next time you need pencils, you need to tell your mom by when you need them and the type or how you need them. This will not only help you get your pencils, but it will show your concern for your mom's effort and time, acknowledging that she goes to school and works, leaving her only the weekends for shopping.

So I should have told my mom last weekend that I needed pencils for that Tuesday. The type of pencil is easy. Definitely not those silly "Hello Kitty" or "Bratz" pencils, or any cute, pink pencil. Give me a straight yellow, number 2 pencil. Another lesson for my Opportunity Manual.

When you ask for something or for HELP -a request- don't FORGET to say by -WHEN- and -HOW- Failing to do so may result in having to do your homework with crayons

Now that I knew how to make a request, specifying the time and providing the details of what I want, I told my mom that next Friday I need to make a ship in celebration of the sea. I told my mom that my ship will have shiny lights and little blue windows. *Mami* and *papi* each will need to put aside 3 hours, *mami* for shopping and *papi* for helping me make the ship. They should be happy, no complaints, since I couldn't have made my request any clearer, right?

I was getting so good at this "making effective requests" thing, that I started to notice when others around me were making ineffective requests. I was surprised that even people that I looked up to, like Mrs. Lee, were often indirect about saying what they really wanted. Adults love to say: "Let's have lunch some time," and yet they never say when or where. What's the point?

And, of course, I could no longer standby and watch Natsuki hold back when she had so much to say, like the day we had a class on world beliefs, and Mrs. Lee asked if anyone knew anything about Japanese values. Natsuki raised her hand so slightly that Mrs. Lee didn't even notice. The *Comadres* were getting ready to speak when I had to step in and take action— an INTERVENTION! Other than their taste for California rolls, what can the *Comadres* possibly know about Japanese values? Just before one of Kelly Lopez' protegés could get a word in, I tickled Natsuki's ribs and her hand flew way up high.

"Yes Natsuki?," asked our teacher.

Natsuki surprised everyone with a detailed speech on her beloved culture. When she sat down, she looked straight at me and growled.

"What did you that for? Poking my ribs? Really, Javi?"

"Natsuki, my friend," I responded with my new found Zen calmness, "if you want to ask for something, you must communicate, express yourself clearly so others will understand what you want."

She tried to hold her frown, but it quickly gave way to a half-smile. That day we walked home together.

NEWSFLASH
Unless you're under six years old NO ONE can read your MIND
Silence is your biggest enemy

Chapter 5
The Transparent Blurter

I threw myself wholeheartedly into preparing flyers, following Benjy's example. The success of Beny's guitar classes continued to inspire me. I even stepped oustide of my "comfort zone" by trying to make the flyers look pretty—clearly not my style, but I was sure they would draw lots of attention.

"Will you help me pass out flyers so that people will sponsor me for tennis camp?," l asked Mrs. Lee, with every ounce of courage in my body.

Mrs. Lee stared at me with her moon-like eyes. I stood firm, drawing a large smile that showed my "whitey-whites." I couldn't have looked any more sincere at that moment.

But I didn't receive the enthusiasm I was expecting from Mrs. Lee.

"Javi, you play tennis?," she asked as she hastily slid the flyer in the top drawer of her desk.

And that was only the first of her line of questioning. The flyers were pretty, I looked sincere, what exactly was the problem?

It seemed as if all my hard work all those years at school weren't paying off when it came to raising funds for tennis camp. Why all the questions? Didn't Mrs. Lee know who I was? I was starting to get the feeling that my family was a mystery to Mrs. Lee. I know *mami* can't make it to the PTA meetings, but what about MY accomplishments? And Mrs. Lee wasn't the only one questioning me. Everyone I made the flyer request to asked me a bunch of questions or they blew me off. No one believed that I could play tennis. Didn't they remember how fast I could run? Or that I can jump as high as a kangaroo? Hadn't I shown what I was capable of?

"Yeah, you're capable, Javi. Capable of falling! Besides, I just don't see you wearing a tennis skirt. You're too much of a tomboy," Kelly Lopez grinned as she cursed me into tomboy-land forever.

I don't know where things went so haywire with Kelly. She seems set on putting me down lately. We were good friends in first and second grade. Maybe she's still upset about the "Presidential Challenge Award"?

She hasn't been the same since.

But it wasn't just Kelly and Mrs. Lee who doubted me. My best friend Natsuki also questioned my tennis camp intentions.

"Javi," she said, moving her right finger towards her mouth, "I don't think I have ever seen you actually play tennis."

Now a thousand thoughts scattered through my hard head. Natsuki might be my best friend, but she doesn't know EVERYTHING I like to do, we're not the same. Of course, I should have kept this thought to myself, but this is my weakness, you see. I'm not very good at keeping my thoughts to myself. I am a blurter. That's right. A transparent blurter—I hide nothing!

"What about you, Natsuki?" I snapped at her after a long day of feeling battered to pieces. "What do you like to do? I know you take piano classes because you like to please your teacher! I just don't get it! Who takes classes just to hang out with their teacher?"

As the argument between Natsuki and I became even more heated, my chances of getting any help from anyone, especially from Mrs. Lee, faded quickly. Mrs. Lee left school without a word about my flyer to anyone that day. Kelly started spreading a rumor that I wanted to go tennis camp just to join forces with the *Comadres*. Worse yet, Natsuki didn't speak to me for the rest of the day. That was no fun at all.

Kelly and her *Comadres* all played with their new gadgets in the "it" part of the yard during recess. Natsuki quietly made drawings that she wouldn't share with anybody, especially me. A flood of sadness washed over me.

Was I missing something? Was my request to be sponsored

not effective? Maybe there was something to this whole communication thing I was just not getting.

I asked my parents for *Tío* Bill's number and called him that evening after dinner. *Tío* Bill questioned and questioned me and finally let out a long sigh. He paused for a few moments.

"Communication can be tricky. There are many types of requests, Javi. In some instances, such as when you ask for a glass of water, it's obvious to people why it is important to you. It sounds like, in the case of sponsoring you for tennis camp, it's not so obvious why this is important to you, or to anyone sponsoring you, for that matter."

Now I felt confused. Was I supposed to explain to everyone why I wanted to go to tennis camp? That sounded like a lot of work!

"No Javi, you don't always need to explain every detail to everyone. But others must feel that they are a part of something when they sponsor you. Another way to think about this is by thinking of what you are OFFERING. This is another form of communicating that I learned in my class on entrepreneurship."

Offering? That's another big word. Geez, how many more words are there?

"You're asking people to sponsor you, to give you money for something, but they don't understand why it matters to you, or why it should matter to them. If you were a well-known tennis pro, your offer might simply be something like offering the pleasure of contributing to your performance—they would feel a part of it. It sounds like, in your case, what you are offering just isn't clear. This is a tricky one, Javi. But I'm sure you'll work something out."

Now I had a lot to think about. I don't think I've ever been good at telling people what they want to hear. Dimitry Skakakun is an expert at telling people EXACTLY what they want to hear.

I was better at the opposite: I somehow manage to say exactly the thing that no one wants to hear, like the time *mami* asked me how she looked in her new pants and I said that her rear looked bigger. (I thought I was pointing out the obvious, but *mami* didn't feel the same way).

I thanked *Tío* Bill, but I wasn't really sure what for yet. It was time for sleep and a big day the next day. This communication stuff really is tricky. I quickly jotted down what he said so I wouldn't forget it.

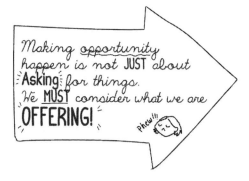

Making opportunity happen is not JUST about Asking for things. We MUST consider what we are OFFERING! Phew!!!

We need to COMMUNICATE to people WHY something is important to US: why we are asking for their HELP

Chapter 6
The Secret Ingredient

Tío Bill gave me a new word to think about: Offer. But I couldn't wrap my head around it yet. There was only one person I knew who could help me now: Benji. I walked by the gym after school and found him and his friends practicing a new song his Uncle Rodrigo had written. Benji announced that his Uncle Rodrigo used to be a "punk rocker" back in the 80's, so the song was suppose to sound a bit like punk rock (although I am not quite sure what punk rock sounds like and I don't think anyone else knew either). But some of the other boys in the band were from Mexico; they claimed to like "Mexican *ranchero*" music (another sound I am not *familiar* with). Whatever it was, it must have been a funny mix between the two. I guess they still hadn't found their sound, but that didn't discourage them. They looked like they were having a heck of a time.

I noticed that when one of the boys made a mistake and hit the wrong note, Benji had a nice way of correcting them. Maybe I could learn something more from Benji about working with people. Gee whiz! I had a lot to learn.

There was a group of kids standing around them. Everybody was interested in the music. Dave, a kid three years younger than Benji, shouted "See you in guitar class at 5:00." Benji winked and gave him a loud "high five."

It became obvious to me that everyone wanted to feel connected to Benji's band somehow. The kids taking guitar classes also felt "part of something." My big hard head, finally understood that Benji was offering the kids more than just a class. (I'm slow to get things through my thick skull, but when I get it, I really get it!) Benji seemed to really understand what kids wanted to connect to.

Benji and I hung out for a while after school. I wanted to ask him so many questions, but I had to keep my cool so as not to bore him too much. So the first thing I did was ask him about his black-and-white guitar.

"I bought this guitar with the money I made mowing my neighbor's lawn," he said, winding up one of the guitar strings, "washing my grandparent's car and helping my mom make runs to the supermarket on my bike."

"How did you come up with that?" I asked.

"I don't know. I guess because no one else was doing those things." He replied.

Benji seemed aware of his surroundings—more than I had ever been. This was something for me to think about, but I had another question.

"How did you know to charge $5.00?"

Benji smiled. He put his guitar back in the case and turned to me, this time with a serious look.

"Look, it's better to pay $5 for a half-hour than to pay $30. That's what my parents paid my guitar instructor. And besides, most kids who want guitar lessons aren't really sure they even like playing guitar yet. They're just trying it out."

What a genius Benji was turning out to be! It finally hit me why everyone was so crazy about his guitar classes and how he was able to get teachers working for him. He had come up with an OFFER. And what an offer it was! Kids change their mind all the time about what activities they like. Parents must get tired of forking over money for lessons every time a kid wants to take up a new activity. Since my parents almost never paid for anything for me, this was all very new to me. Forking over $30 per class just to find out that guitar is just a passing hobby is something parents might not want to get themselves into. But what if they don't do it and end up killing a kid's dreams forever? What if the kid did have an iota of talent, but his or her parents just never gave them a chance? Bingo! That's where Benji's classes come in. Benji gives the kids a taste of what the guitar feels like. Parents pay a small amount. If the kid is really serious, the parents can "upgrade," get the kid a real guitar teacher. If the kid isn't serious, the parents don't lose that much, and even better, they don't have to walk around feeling guilty for the rest of their lives. Now that's an OFFER!

I could finally see it and feel it. Benji's offer wasn't just one that attracted kids and helped them feel connected to cool guitar bands—it was an offer for the parents as well, since it helped them feel better about themselves. So an offers helps someone feel better about themselves, too! That's why the teachers were happy to pass out flyers. They were offering something of value to the parents, and something that also made them feel more valuable.

My Opportunity Manual owed a lot to Benji. It was time to jot down some notes for my Manual.

opportunities arise when we make **OFFERS** that bring VALUE to others

People value something that help them feel BETTER about THEMSELVES

Chapter 7
The Power of Empathy

I went to school the next day with a new outlook on things. This idea of OFFERS that bring something valuable to others stuck with me all day. I started to OBSERVE opportunities.

During lunch, I participated in a little bit of research. I walked by the teachers lounge and noticed that most of the teachers were eating plain sandwiches. I peaked through the office window for a few minutes before Mrs. Lee looked up and saw me.

I'd seen my teachers eating their sandwiches many times, but I hadn't OBSERVED their faces before. Mrs. Lee frowned while biting into what appeared to be a basic ham-and-yellow-cheese-on-white-bread sandwich. She seemed to be eating just to get it over with, rather than enjoying her meal. I noticed that she ate half the sandwich and threw out the rest.

She didn't seem to enjoy her meal. It looked as if Mrs. Lee was eating just to get full before going back to class. Her face wrinkled up when she took the first bite. Other teachers were doing the same as Mrs. Lee. Only one had bothered to microwave her meal before eating part of it and throwing the rest out. What about all those lectures on nutrition? Wasn't it as important for teachers to eat well as it was for kids?

It occurred to me that I could ask Mrs. Lee why she threw her sandwich out. Would she be mad or offended? I didn't want to walk in and interrupt my teachers' private time. So I waited patiently outside the teachers' lounge as I worked up the courage to ask Mrs. Lee about her lunch experience. I hoped I wouldn't offend her, but I had to know why she threw out half her sandwich. I'd never been one to hold back on asking questions. And I've never been very discrete, so when Ms. Mrs. Lee walked out of the lunch room, I took the plunge and asked.

"Mrs. Lee," I approached her with a serious, formal tone of voice, "May I ask you something?"

Mrs. Lee knew I was up to something. She sighed and turned her head away from me while mumbling:

"What's going on, Javi?"

"I noticed that you threw out half you sandwich. Were you not hungry or did you not like it?"

Mrs. Lee suddenly loosened up as she now turned towards me. It seems people like it when you show a sincere interest in their lives.

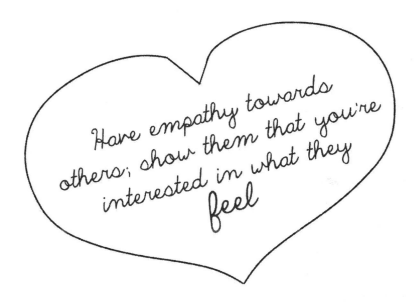

Have empathy towards others; show them that you're interested in what they feel

I think adults call this "empathy." I wasn't sure what "empathy" meant until now, even though Mrs.Lee had us read a book on it. Maybe it's something I should try more often!

"You know, Javi," she said, still looking somewhat shocked by my question, "most teachers don't have time to cook every day. And some of us just lack the imagination to invent new meals. I guess I wasn't really in the mood for a bologna-and-cheese sandwich today."

I felt bad for Mrs. Lee: teachers teaching on an empty stomach.

What a sad picture!

I couldn't help but think about how, in my house, there's always lots of scrumptious food, and I always have tasty goodies that my *papi* makes me for my school lunch.

My *papi* loves to cook. He especially likes cooking different Latino recipes, such as Spanish *Tortilla*, Chilean *Empanadas*, and Mexican *Tortas*. *Papi* has dreamed of having his own food business for some time. He says he's grateful for his job as an accountant, but food is his true calling. *Papi* has an old food stand he purchased once at a garage sale. He was so excited the day he got it, he said it was the real deal, a professional food stand he was able to buy from someone who was going back to his home country—it was never even used! *Mami* and I kept waiting for him to do something with it, but as time passed, he

74

never launched his food businesss. I don't know why he doesn't go for it. He makes tasty food. And all my aunts and uncles seem to enjoy his food.

So he must have something that they really value. Isn't that an OFFER?

Papi giggles every time I mention the subject. After school, I mentioned it once again.

"*Mija* (which means something like "my daughter" in Spanish), one can't make a whole business with just your family as customers, it takes more than that."

So, if we have something valuable that others may like, don't we have an offer there?

Papi always laughs at me when I bring up the subject. I mentioned it again after school, at suppertime.

"No, *mija*, this is just a hobby."

"But you might succeed, *Papi*," I said in my most convincing voice possible.

"Your cooking is great! I bet you can get more customers than just family, *Papi*. Why not give it a go?"

"Javi, you're just a child. You wouldn't understand. It takes a lot more to build a business than you could ever imagine."

Does it really? I never said it was easy, but why did I believe it possible? I thought to myself long and hard over the next couple of days. The image of teachers teaching on an empty stomach stayed with me.

I remember visiting my cousin Claudio in Latin America once and noticing that there were food stands on many corners. Here I've seen some food stands in the *barrios*, the Latino neighborhoods. But there are none where I live. Oh, except for the big coffee stands outside of shopping malls. Those ones look really nice, but they don't sell that much food.

What makes some food stands do better than others? This is a question for the proud owners of food stands in Latin America. I remember that those guys are willing to talk to anyone who will listen. Again, if you don't know something, then ask questions. So far, this questioning thing is working out pretty well. So who will ask the questions? I'm sure my dear cousin Claudio would be willing to help me.

Dear Claudio,

How are things going with you? If you need anything from the States, I'd be more than happy to help. Well, at least I hope the Opportunity Manual will be of help to you.

Speaking of the Opportunity Manual, I'm still trying to figure out how to make opportunity happen. I've been thinking of *papi* and his cooking skills. Why not consider starting up a food stand, a "*carrito,*" right here where I live? I know it may seem strange to think about a *carrito* stand in this neighborhood; after all, people here buy their fast food at fast food places, malls, or the corner store. Still, I have fond memories of walking in the neighborhood in the middle of the day and eating a *torta* at your local *carrito* stand. Can you do me a favour and talk to the *carrito* stands in your neighborhood? Are there some that do better than others? Why are people more willing to go to one stand over another? I hope these questions don't seem silly. My head is spinning a thousand miles a minute with this opportunity business.

Thanks, *primo*. You're a life saver!

Javi.

8 hours and 45 minutes later

Hey Javi!!!!

Hi, *prima*. I took a ride on my bike around the neighborhood and where my *mami* works, with my friends and my little sister. I spoke with every *carrito* owner I could find, and you're right, there is one that stands out above the rest: *Tortas La Doña*. Whereas everyone else is charging the same 10 pesos for a *torta*, (you know, those big, elaborate sandwich-like things filled with all kinds of meats, cheeses, cream, avocado), I met one couple, *Don Manuel* and *Doña Luisa*, who charged 30 pesos, and they're the most successful of all. There are lines around the corner for their *tortas*. They've saved enough money to send both of their kids to the university. I spoke to a few of their customers, who really seemed to be enjoying their meal. Why are they willing to pay 20 pesos more? They say it's because they feel they are getting a quality meal.

When I went to the other stands, I asked some folks who walked by whether they buy there, and they looked at me ashamed. "Sometimes we eat there, but we feel bad afterwards because we don't really know what we're eating." The couples' stand actually lists the brand names of the cold cuts and ingredients they use. Their *tortas* are much bigger, the *bolillo* bread is crispier and fresher, and they offer many choices of ingredients. People line up at all hours of the day while taking a stroll in the neighborhood. I asked why they can't make them at home. They said It gives them a chance to leave the house, to take a break. Also, *Tortas* La Doña is always introducing new flavors, new sauces, and they have unique ways of mixing ingredients.

Well, *prima*, I hope this helps you. I know I feel inspired. Thanks for the great questions. Before, I thought all of these places were the same, and that there wasn't much of a future in small business. Now I see that having one's own business can be cool!

Un abrazo,

Your *primo*

Claudio

send

Time to reflect: Woooooow! I am impressed. Asking questions sure seems to work!

My dad was super right. You need more than family members to start a business. And *Tortas La Doña* is a great example of that; besides, they're doing something better—bringing VALUE to others. People feel good about themselves eating there. Maybe because they get bored eating at home or they just need a break from work, taking a breath of fresh air.

For the first time since I began this adventure, I had a plan. I love the sound of that, especially because it involves my dad. He says he loves watching me cook, teaching me how to do it and eating what we make together. He says we grow closer when we cook, although each time I want to change the recipe, leave out the olive or use a different cheese, like havarti, he gives me a strange look.

"Why does an *empanada* have an olive and a hard-boiled egg?," I asked my *papi* that afternoon.

"That's the recipe," he said very seriously.

It was as if the recipe was his history. I don't know why people in my family are so bound to traditions. I don't think it would be the end of the world if I used green pepper just once, instead of onion.

Or would it?

Let's get back to reality, please. I have to stick to my plan. I'm going to take my dad's little old stand, my mom's heat-storing plates, and I'm going to OFFER some *empanadas* and *tortillas* at lunchtime. That way, I can save up for tennis camp!

So what have I learned?

Chapter 8

The Lactose Incident

The little stand was a challenge. The school had given us permission to set up outside after class, but only for one month. In order to stay any longer, the food had to be really good—not just tasty. Parents, teachers, and of course, kids, all had to like it. It was a fair deal, and I was ready for a CHALLENGE!

There were a few things I hadn't worked out. So first I asked my *mami* for some help.

"*Mami*, would you help me set prices for the food? I'm a little confused."

My *mami* didn't know what to say at first—she thought about it all the way home. Luckily, she had the same consultant as me, my *Tío* Bill. We called him and invited him to taste the yummy products and after that he sat down with us and started to think.

We saw him smiling again, although he was kind of tired because he had just got back from his course on entrepreneurship. He gave us a lecture while he ate a meat *empanada*.

"The truth is," he said, "you'll have to wait and see how much people are willing to pay. If you raise the prices, less people will be able to buy, and your sales will fall. But if you lower them too much, people won't believe that your food is good—they'll think you use bad ingredients. The worse part is that you won't be able to cover your costs."

Tío Bill sat down with us and we estimated the cost of each *empanada* and *tortilla*. We calculated something called the "margin," which is everything you charge beyond the cost; in other words, my tennis camp money. Now I understand what math is for!

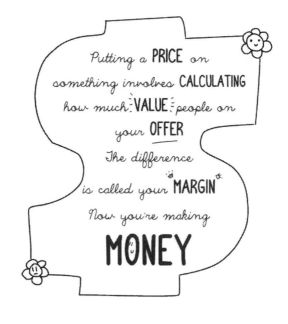

Putting a **PRICE** on something involves **CALCULATING** how much **VALUE** people on your **OFFER**

The difference is called your **MARGIN**

Now you're making

MONEY

The first day was kind of busy. Most parents and teachers had never tasted a Chilean *empanada*. But nothing worried me more than the "olive factor." What would they say when they bit into their *empanada* and found an olive?

But the truth was that things were going well. Parents and teachers were liking the *empanadas*, while kids preferred the Spanish *tortilla*. Parents said that the combination of potatoes and eggs seemed healthy, as well as a good alternative to the hamburgers, chips and hot dogs they usually ate before they got home.

It's surprising how many people gave the stand a chance. I didn't receive one complaint. Maybe it was too soon to cry "victory". But things were moving so fast that I had to hire Natsuki, since I couldn't prepare and mind the register at the same time. I was surprised to see how organized and efficient she was. Everybody said so. Interesting skills that this girl had, why hadn't I noticed them before?

My parents were very clear that after working at the stand, I had to do my homework, just like any other day. That was fine with me.

☆ ☆ ☆

One very hot afternoon, Natsuki and I were feeling super lazy, so we didn't open the stand. What is the worst that could happen?

I found out that people had been waiting for our delicious food. What had we done!?

The next day, people were complaining a lot, as if we had missed an important class, or cheated on a test. But I realized that when you work on something like this, you have to be consistent, like in a race. You can't just stop and eat a hot dog during a marathon!

I was going to have to take this more seriously if I wanted to reach my goal. "You have to excel at your commitments,"

Mrs. Lee said, reminding me that otherwise people at school wouldn't take me seriously. Was that possible? I'm very serious! Who could doubt it? We wouldn't let them down again.

And we kept our promise: every day we'd open on time, and then, when we closed, we left the stand there, tied to a pole.

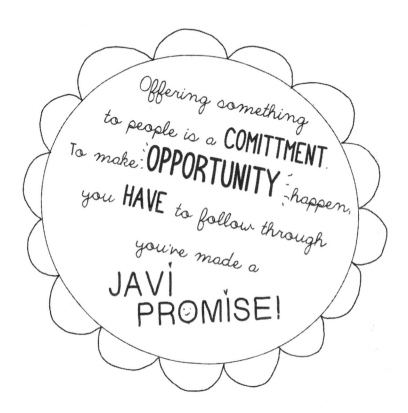

Offering something to people is a COMITTMENT. To make OPPORTUNITY happen, you HAVE to follow through you've made a JAVI PROMISE!

Natsuki helped me put my mom's plates back, along with everything we could take home: wrappers, napkins and all that stuff, as well as the food, of course. Sometimes, she seems to be two different girls. One is shy and mysterious; the other is like the captain of a ship, more organized than I am. Which was the real one? I wondered, but there were more important things to worry about.

My mom helped, too. She was happy to help after her classes at the state school.

Suddenly, something terrible happened. After two weeks of tasting my "exotic" delicious, food –as hard as it was for me to believe– people seemed to grow tired of it. Our sales began to slow down, and what had seemed to be my path to success assumed the stride of a crippled turtle.

By the third week, I was feeling exhausted, and I wasn't saving enough money for tennis camp. I was f-a-i-l-i-n-g, horror of horrors! At the end of each day, I had a lot of leftover *empanadas* and *tortillas*, to the delight of the only truly faithful customers I had left: the neighborhood dogs and cats.

I was getting more and more frustrated. Everything I did seemed to backfire. I even took it out on poor, loyal Natsuki. She gave a customer a cheese *empanada*, when she had asked for one with meat. Aw, but that wasn't the worst part of it: it turns out that this customer was lactose-intolerant and had already bit into a piece. Her face turned purple, and then her stomach swole. To make things worse, Natsuki then offered her a glass of milk instead of water.

AAAAAHHHH!

Of course, with my luck, things could always get worse.

It turns out the woman was Kelly López' mom. Kelly saw everything, and it was just the ammunition she longed for.

Kelly had already been pressuring me about the stand. During gym class, she turned to me in front of the other girls and, with those nervous eyes and turned-up nose of hers, looked at me and said:

"Javi," she said as if she was giving a speech, "I thought you were a real student, an athlete and had a great future. Why are you going around being a worker? Our parents didn't come to this country for you to be doing such lowly tasks. You have to forget that dirty, sad work, ASAP, at least if you want to keep being friends with us… Do you get what I'm saying Javi?"

I did not let Kelly's threats get to me. I mean, I was earning money and making people happy—at least I thought so. I loved my little stand, I had no complaints. Of course, until that day, the darkest day of creation. The day of the LACTOSE INCIDENT, the day when the innocent teeth of Kelly's mom sank into an *empanada* full of greasy cheese, instead of a meat *empanada*. If only we could erase that Lactose Incident. Phew, but nobody knows how to do that yet—time-travel, I mean.

Kelly López had a good pair of lungs, and on that terrible day she used them to shout at me very loudly.

"What are you doing?" she screamed, with a fury I'd never heard before. "Are you trying to kill my mom?!"

When her mom returned to the scene and was breathing normally, she looked at her daughter and stopped her in her tracks.

"That's enough, Angélica Pascualina López!," she said forcefully.

The other kids didn't even know that this girl's real name was Angélica Pascualina. Kelly now looked at me even more furiously, as if millions of fires were raging inside her.

Kelly got her revenge: she marched straight to the principal's office. Benji, the teachers and other children had also gathered to see what was going on. I didn't like what was happening at all. I had less than one week to go before the trial month was over.

The principal was hard on me. She stood in front of me, straight as a tree.

"Give me a list of the ingredients you're using," she said very harshly, as if I were selling nuclear weapons.

I heard the other kids whispering. "She probably uses expired foods," "she probably spits on them." But the worst of them all was Kelly, who took over the scene and pointed her finger at me.

"Tell her to show us her license or permit thingy to sell food!"

My what? I had no idea that I needed a permit!

"Javi," the principal began, "you have to handle your business more professionally, this doesn't seem right to me."

Those were her last words. I felt hurt, betrayed and exhausted. I felt defeated. I thought I was making everyone happy, but I was wrong. Even worse still: they accused me of being unprofessional.

"Natsuki," I said furiously and unfairly, "what in the world were you thinking? You gave Kelly's mom a cheese *empanada*! Not only that, you gave her a glass of milk! This is all YOUR fault!"

I was attacking her, but Natsuki didn't just stand there. All those weeks of hard work, responsibility and serving people had changed her. She didn't sit still and keep quiet like before. She had a lot to say.

"Javi," she said, putting her hands on her waist, "the stand has been slow all week, everybody already tried the *empanadas*. You say they're delicious and healthy, but people can't eat greasy cheese and meat with dough all the time. I can't stand any more of that food, that's why I bring my sushi rolls in my lunchbox!"

She showed me: she had little balls of rice of different sizes, and they looked totally delicious.

"Pay attention," Natsuki continued, taking the bull by its horns, "just because you love *empanadas* and *tortilla*, that doesn't mean we're all going to think the same way. This is certainly not my fault! Yes, I made a mistake… I'm sorry, but that didn't make you lose the stand. You did that all by yourself. Maybe you haven't noticed, but I was only trying to help you. Though you make it really hard."

Natsuki put her left arm on my shoulder, her face expressing more sadness than anger at that moment.

"I was happy to see you take initiative and start the stand. But you know what? With all that has happened, I am starting to think that maybe you just want to make easy money. You haven't put your heart into the stand. This is all just for tennis camp, isn't it?"

I answered with silence.

"I don't even know why you want to go there," Natsuki continued, "you're a good athlete, but this whole thing has made you very OPPORTUNISTIC."

Ow, that really hurt. I thought she would be loyal with me until the end, right? That's what best friends are for. Now she was giving me a very clear message: that I'm a greedy girl, or something like that. Easy money?

The truth is, I didn't have the faintest idea what being OPPORTUNISTIC meant. It sounded bad—worse than bad, it sounded like a terrible insult. But if there was one thing I knew for sure, arguing with Natsuki was really dumb, simply because she knew more words than any other kid in my class.

I had the hunch that my best friend was accusing me of being

a bad person. And that hurt as if an arrow had been thrust
through my heart.

I was as alone as can be: I was out of Kelly López' circle, and it
would take some time for Natsuki to forgive me, if she ever did.
And there was a more urgent issue: I needed a permit for my
little stand? I was ready to throw in the towel and head towards
the desert. But what kind of story would this be if I had given
up?

What I needed was to release some energy, I was sure of that. I
found some older kids on my block.

"What do you want, Javi?," asked one.

I smiled: they knew me, and if I was there, it was only for one
reason.

"What do you think?" I replied with a challenging tone, "To
run, what else?"

It had been a few weeks since we had competed. I had put all my energy into the little stand and my obsession with tennis camp. Aaron Scott was 13 years old, but he had always been shorter than me, and he was always ready for a good competition. He said I beat him because I was taller than him. But Aaron had grown in the last couple months. We were almost the same height now.

We ran around the whole block twice, tying both times. Breathless, my rival approached me.

"Well, Javi," he said, breathing very heavily, "you've been a great competitor, but soon I'll be bigger than you, and I'll beat you."

I smiled, because I really didn't care.

"Whatever! Then I'll have one year to catch up to you, dude" I said, happier than I'd been in a long time.

Home, sweet home.

☆ ☆ ☆

I had to close the stand for a week. I had to organize my ideas and think about how to fix things. I needed to look for help in the only place that couldn't let me down: my family. Specifically my *papi* and my *Tío* Bill.

"Hey, kiddo!," said *Tío* Bill, "How are things going?"

My uncle had never seen me truly sad. He grabbed me with his big hands and lifted me until I was facing him.

"Are you all right? You look a little yellow!"

I told him what had happened with the little stand, with Natsuki and with the great López family. He told me that all businesses have "breakdowns", when things just don't work as well. When things are working well, you don't notice what

98

needs to improve, until things don't work.

"Open your eyes wide," he said, "and OBSERVE carefully, pay attention to how people respond to what you are offering, even if they aren't complaining. Understood? Not everyone complains when they don't like something. Most of the time, they don't say anything; they simply stop buying the product. You have to ask questions and LISTEN".

OBSERVE? All that stuff about being alert, perceiving, and OBSERVING seemed something really important, but I wasn't sure what it meant yet.

"Don't worry," he said. "Maybe you should even thank Kelly and Natsuki for what they've taught you."

What? Thank Kelly López? That was an idea I would never have come up with. UG! Sometimes my uncle tells me such strange things.

Over the next few days, I thought a lot about my good friend, the girl who brought her hidden sushi: Natsuki. I knew she was super-mega-hyper right about everything she had said, that the *empanada* and *tortilla* fever had passed.

My mistake was thinking that, just because I had overcome the Olive Factor, people were enjoying my food enough to buy them every single day. Now I see that I should have asked people what they thought, and if they had any ideas for improving my little stand.

Natsuki had done me a tremendous favour after all, because she'd been the only one to tell me what I was doing wrong. That was what Tio Bill was trying to tell me.

"She gave you an assessment," he said, "You know what that is?"

I looked at him for the 10 longest seconds of my life. Did I know what an assessment was? I wanted to say yes, but I didn't know.

"No," I answered, ashamed of not knowing.

"That's OK," he said, "Look, assessments are things that people think but don't always say. Sometimes they hurt, it's true, but we shouldn't always take them so personally---they are just what the person is thinking, their opinion, at that moment. It does not mean that the opinion is one hundred percent true. If you think about it, it is an opportunity to improve what we're doing."

Wow, I thought. This is going to have to sink in for a while. So Natsuki gave me an assessment—that I was being opportunistic and not putting enough dedication into the stand. How could I be more like the stand Claudio spoke about, *Tortas La Doña*. Darn! I see now that my little stand didn't even have a name. How could I have been so distracted? Maybe Natsuki was right and I wasn't putting enough heart into this.

It's time for a PAUSE: I have to think.

observe and listen
to people: BEYOND
what they SAY
when in DOUBT
ASK and LISTEN!

Don't take assessments personally—learn from these and GET BACK on the HORSE!

Chapter 9

The Wasabi Experiment

I think *mami* felt real bad because of what happened at my food stand, but what bothered her most was my argument with Natsuki. It was strange for her to be interested, but apparently she valued our friendship a lot. *Mami* was always so busy that I thought she didn't notice these types of things; or that she simply didn't care. And now she was telling me that friends are important! For the first time, my mom was meddling in my business—I was happy to see this new side of my *mami*.

"Javi," she said confidently, "what if we call Natsuki and you go stay the night at her house?"

WHAT? Had I heard right? She was really making me feel wheezy. Literally, in my surprised daze I tripped over my own left foot. Like I said before, *mami* never let me stay over at

103

anybody's house. I didn't want to ask her anything else, since I was afraid she might change her mind.

A smile finally crossed my lips, the same one that also lit up my *mami's* pretty face. Maybe it was time to insist on the tennis thing, too? No, Javi, don't press your luck, one victory at a time.

"I'm impressed at what you've achieved with that little stand," she said while she arranged my uncombed hair with her hand. "You know? I'm glad you succeeded with your project."

The truth is, she was secretly happy that the little stand was moving forward. *Papi's* old dream was alive! The poor thing had been sitting in the backyard for a long time, and I saw how it ruined *mami's* garden, flattening some plants, and casting shadows over others.

105

My *mami* and Natsuki's parents agreed on me staying the night, but there was still the issue of settling things between the two of us.

"Natsuki?," I called her on the telephone, afraid of what she might say.

She took a while to answer. At first I thought she was being shy, but then I realized she had something in her mouth.

"Javi!," she said joyfully, "my mom said she talked to your mom and that you're coming over."

Yet another surprise. Natsuki had already forgotten the incident. Was I really on another planet? Maybe I was the alien and I had switched over to another dimension. Once again, I felt like I was telling jokes to myself, and I let out a little giggle.

Natsuki smiled back, I could hear her through the receiver. I felt relieved, as if a great weight had been taken off my shoulders.

"What are you waiting for, come over?," she said.

I had dinner with Natsuki and her parents, Mr. and Mrs. Tanaka. I had never tasted Japanese food, except for a California roll or something like that. There were some very nice rice balls, some had crabmeat, avocado and cucumber. It was all seriously delicious, yummy-yummy. The chicken teriyaki and the salad with yuzo sauce were my absolute favorites.

"Are you sure you've never had Japanese food?," Mrs. Tanaka asked when she saw how eagerly I was swallowing my food.

After my friend's parents went to bed, we stayed awake real late. It was time for an EXPERIMENT, as Natsuki called it. We were going to do something very crazy, even for me! We were going on a journey to the strange frontiers of Japanese food.

We went to a cabinet where there were several jars with names I'd never heard of, parading in front of us like an army of flavors.

"We've got soy sauce," Natsuki began to list them, "ginger, sukyaki sauce, low-sodium soy sauce, tamari sauce, ponzu sauce, yuzo sauce, teriyaki sauce, eel sauce and WASABI."

"Wa-what?"

"Wasabi."

"Oh," I said, but I had no idea what that strange green stuff was.

She smiled a sly smile. We had a lot to learn yet. She taught me how to make the little rice balls, rolling them up with that black seaweed—what was it called? Oh, yeah: nori! We had to cook a lot of rice, because we were always running out. Our inventions were getting bigger and bigger.

Something inside me had changed: cooking wasn't just a means to an end. There was something alive in the art of creating things to eat. Yes, cooking mattered to me now.

Natsuki took a little ground beef and placed it in something she called a "gyoza" with sukyaki sauce. I didn't know there were also Japanese *empanadas*. Another one of Natsuki'a secrets! I'd been blind to all these things, maybe it was because I didn't know how to OBSERVE.

It turns out that my friend wasn't only good with food. Natsuki also had a good instinct for sales. She had been selling food and other things of Japanese origin, but she hadn't told anyone at school. Mr. and Mrs. Tanaka belonged to the city's Japanese chamber of commerce. They participated in fairs and exhibits where the community sold its products. But she didn't just trade with her parents around. You see, Natsuki is a fan of Manga, which is the name for Japanese comics and also animation from her country of origin. So she dresses up in a traditional kimono and heads to their conventions. Selling ramen, sobu noodles and sweet balls. She makes a lot of money. And she didn't just sell—Natsuki acted, too!

Natsuki in Kimono

I shouldn't be so quick to judge others, as I had Natsuki. After all, there is more to a person than meets the eye. Besides, people change all the time.

"Japanese food isn't just delicious," said Natsuki, "it requires concentration and love. Things have to look nice, they have to be delicious to look at."

"What do you mean?"

She began to roll a roll, but it wasn't just any roll: she used avocado, cucumber, kanikama, and, to my surprise, she added mango. When she showed me the finished product, it was a multicolour food piece, almost like a figure made out of play-dough. But more than anything, it was pretty, attractive to look at.

"See?," she said, "many people know how to make sushi now, but not everyone knows how to make beautiful sushi."

Dedicate yourself with seriousness to executing your OFFER! Your offer needs to be DIFFERENT from the REST !!!

I now understood: there were three things that she was teaching me now, ones that she had been trying to to show me when she made her ASSESSMENT of my behaviour. You had to dedicate yourself to something with honesty and seriousness, it was important to respect whatever you're doing, and, finally, you had to be different. Great lessons! And they had been right in front of me the whole time.

I was having so much fun learning about my friend's sushi ability that I didn't notice what I was putting in my mouth. Some sauces were sweet, others were salty, but I didn't even notice when I put that mysterious green stuff into my mouth: wasabi. The champion of champions in spicy foods, that was one of the things I wish I'd known beforehand.

Natsuki's parents walked in and saw the scene. I'll never forget the look on Mr. Tanaka's face, which could be summed up as: "Whaaaaat?"

Mom Tanaka was more understanding and laughed a lot with us. But she need not say no more. Natsuki understood the message: clean the kitchen, and that's what we did. Even more than that: we made breakfast for everyone. It was great to eat noodles in the morning. I guess everything worked out fine. Things were finally changing.

While I tasted those new flavors, I got an idea. Why couldn't Chilean food overcome the Olive Factor? I didn't like that idea of following recipes ONLY "by the book" at all. I had learned that cooking was something you have to do with your heart, that it was similar to my other love, sports. You had to challenge yourself and seek excellence, so why not bring in other flavors, other traditions and invent new recipes for the little stand ?

The exploration with Natsuki opened up new doors for me. Let's go inside!

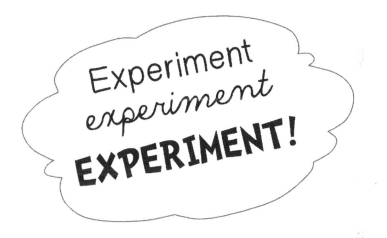

Chapter 10

The Research Mission

Last week I let my mom take me to get a haircut and buy me some dresses. I don't like the whole haircut thing, I always imagine a certain "look" and it never works out like I imagined. My mom likes to give me a French style—you know, a bob cut with bangs like that girl in the movie "Amélie." My mom loves that movie.

"Javi, I think you'd look so cute in a dress."

"You always say that, *mami*."

She looked at me almost as if she were begging, touched my face and used that "little puppy" face that she knows will get to me.

"Do it as a favour, everyone wears a dress once in a while."

Since I couldn't say no, I would use the chance to do some research. That's right, I'd have the chance to observe the food stands, what people were eating, when and how.

The food court is a great mix of smells and flavors, people end up always mixing their foods up. Some were eating Mongolian chicken from the Chinese place with Mexican nachos. Some kids were eating grilled hamburgers and then bought juice from the nature foods stand. People like to mix things up.

There were different flavors: an Italian restaurant, a Chinese one, even one that only sold Tandoori food—chicken and red meats. The lady serving people there explained to me that Tandoori was a type of clay that made the meat turn red. That seemed interesting: the food had a story. On the other hand, I saw that healthy food was very trendy, people were taking care of themselves, which seemed great to me. People ate salads and drank smoothies.

I was so focused on the restaurants that I didn't notice I was on collision course with someone.

"Hey? What are you doing, Javi?," said Benji, with a surprise, "Is your head in the clouds? I have been waving my hand in front of you and you didn't even see me!"

"I'm doing spy work."

"What are you spying on?"

I told him about how I was spying on the restaurants.

"What a crazy girl," said the boy, with an honest surprise on his face. "Yeah, look, this isn't the right place to learn about flavors."

"Why not? It's full of food," I said, but now I was the one who was surprised.

Benji glanced quickly at the restaurants in the mall.

"No, Javi," said Benji, much more confidently than before, "maybe we should visit my Aunt Gloria in the gourmet district. Have you been there?"

I shook my head no. I kind of remembered going there once when I was smaller, but I wasn't sure.

"It's a place in the city," said Benji, who sounded like a professor now, "where you can find the best food in the whole world!"

Then the "on" button switched on inside my head, maybe slowly, like my grandpa's old car. I had to make a request to Benji. Of course, I had gotten better at this requesting stuff, but for some reason, with this boy it was a little harder...

"I want to see your aunt's place, Benji, would you take me there?"

At that moment, I saw his eyes lit up. Maybe (although it seemed unbelievable) I just realized something: he enjoyed my company as much as I enjoyed his. Weird, huh?

"Yeah," he said, surprised, "I'll take you, but what will your parents say? Listen, get their permission and let me know."

Well, he was right: one thing was for Benji to say yes, but something very different was for my dear, but strict *papi*, to say yes. Besides, lately there was something strange going on with him. Maybe he was in a bad mood because of the stand. He didn't feel like making *empanadas*, and we had stopped talking about the little stand. My poor little stand was sitting there, in its old place in the garden, like a reminder that sometimes dreams don't come true.

I knew it wasn't the best moment to do something crazy, but I felt that if I was going to make a change, I had to do it on my own terms. So I said goodbye to Benji, but as I lost sight of him, one thing became very clear to me: I had a new mission.

✮ ✮ ✮

My dad was sitting down, fixing the old telephone. That was another one of his "halfway" hobbies: fixing things that remained broken when he finished working on them. I stood in front of him and gave him what I thought was my best "angel face." But I knew I had a Pandora's box on my hands.

"Focus on your homework, Javi," he said with his serious look, "If you have leftover time, we'll take extra Math classes, or we'll find a good after-school science club."

I was confused. First, he helped me, and then he started talking about Math –besides, I was doing well in that subject–

and Science classes. What had changed, Mr. *Papi*? (puzzled)

"You have to do more extracurricular activities," he said. "One day you're going to be a professional, an accountant, lawyer or engineer, something serious. Cooking is just a hobby, you know that."

I had not expected him to hit me with all of that. What if my dad was right and I was wrong? After all, the cooking thing had come up because of tennis camp—which I hadn't forgotten, of course.

For the following week I put my head so deeply into my books that I began to lose sight of things. I even let my dad convince me to join the "mathletes", the club for all the Math geniuses. I think I really distracted them with all my chatter.

Was this story ready to end? No way! When I visited Natsuki's house, I discovered I was still in the race.

"What if you call Benji?," said my friend suggestively. "I don't think you dare to."

"I will."

"I bet you don't dare tell him to come over."

A challenge, that's what she was throwing at me. I couldn't resist a challenge.

"Of course I'll go," said Benji. "See you at three, all right?"

I said yes, of course. Natsuki jumped up and down eagerly. Wow, too much excitement, huh? Anyway, calling boys, going into the city and escaping adult supervision was new to me. Even though I may pay for it later on, I felt I was doing the right thing: I was fighting for what I believed was the right thing to do.

We met just as we had agreed: at Natsuki's front door. Her parents let her take the bus, so we headed towards the district with all the restaurants and cafes.

The restaurants looked really elegant. Even in the little marketplace we walked through, there was organic food that was really well presented.

But the biggest surprise of all was Aun't Gloria's restaurant: it was truly *fenomenal!*. Until then, I'd never known what that little word that my *mami* always said in Spanish meant. She's really passionate when she wants to be. For her, "*fenomenal*" is more than cool and fantastic together.

"*Fenomenal!*," I said out loud.

What was so incredible about Aunt Gloria's restaurant? Well, there was many things that impressed me. From the color of the walls to the elaborate menu. Aunt Gloria was good-looking: she

119

looked better than many professionals, this place was her dream, and she filled it with elegance, strength and something else: care. Commitment, she said. This was the voice of her soul.

At that moment I understood that my little stand had to succeed. With one more chance, I was sure we could get it right. Looking around Aunt Gloria's restaurant, I couldn't stop dreaming.

I found myself caring less and less about going to summer camp. There was a storm brewing in my heart. This was about starting something. Better yet, this was about becoming an entrepreneur!

When we returned to Natsuki's home, my *papi* found out about our trip to the city, to the neighborhood with the restaurants and everything. I was about to be punished. Maybe I deserved it, but I wasn't afraid.

"*Mija*," he said, uncomfortable with the whole situation, "you never did anything like this to us. You lied to me. Why?"

I hadn't been totally honest with my *papi*. I guess that is because things had been sort of tense at home. But now, he looked really upset. I felt bad about lying to him, but not about going to the city with Benji and Natsuki. Had I asked his permission, he would not have let me go. And I would not have seen Benji's aunt Gloria's *fenomenal* and incredible restaurant.

Papi was comfortable with his way of doing things, even though they didn't make him happy. That's why he didn't change the recipe—he was a man who needed his traditions.

I was locked up for a couple of hours in my room. Of course I wasn't happy, but I wasn't about to start crying. I took advantage of the opportunity and peacefulness of my room to take notes for my Opportunity Manual, but when I was trying to concentrate, my *papi* came into the room. He didn't look calm, happy or at ease. I think he wanted to get out of this situation, but didn't know how.

"You're changing very quickly," he said, sitting down on the side of my bed.

I looked at him. His big eyes were like two big full moons shining on a clear cloudless night.

"*Papi*," I answered, kind of sad because of what I was about to say, "and you're changing too slowly. Your too stuck in your traditions."

I did it: I gave my dad an assessment, like *Tío* Bill had explained to me. He would also give me his assessments. I breathed hard and tried not to take them personally, as *Tío* Bill had taught me.

Papi was trying to help me see the pain that I had caused him by lying to him, and by escaping. Something that I wouldn't even have dared to think about doing before. I said I was sorry, not because I regretted my trip, but simply because lying to my *papi* wasn't right. I knew that.

Receiving assessments wound up being easier than making them. Nobody had ever talked back or confrontational in the Vega household, much less my *papi*. That's how we did things, I know that there's a thin line between making an assessment and disrespecting someone, but I let my instincts and my heart guide me. And I had a secret weapon: 300,000 new ideas.

Maybe because of how much he loves me, he continued listening all the same. I was bombarding him with all my excitement.

"There are many new recipes," I began, announcing my attack, "You know? Food that combines the old and the new. The world is becoming more mixed."

"Where did you get that from?"

"You have to move beyond the Olive Factor," I said, waving my hands in the air like a magician.

"The Olive what?" Asked *papi*.

"You know, the traditional recipe that says you ALWAYS have to use an olive" I protested.

I think I knocked him out with that. I told him about what I had seen at Aunt Gloria's, how the restaurant looked, and about the fantastic menu.

My dad was changing his mind. He had seen some truth in my words, or maybe it was just out of exhaustion. But we were ready: I was back in the race again!

:TEAMWORK:
Means that sometimes
you have to make
ASSESSMENTS of
others, EVEN when you
feel BAD about it

Chapter 11

Back to the Race

Like many things that seemed impossible to me before, getting the food permit turned out to be really simple. It was actually called "a food handlers permit". All we had to do was pay ten dollars and take a two-hour class on Sunday. Dad and Natsuki learned that they shared a pretty nerdy passion for taking scrupulous notes of each of the instructions they gave. Thank God they enjoyed that part, because otherwise I wouldn't have been free for the really fun part.

And what was this fun part for me? Easy: talking to people. Of course, I know everyone thinks I'm a chatterbox, but I was learning to speak more slowly, to listen more attentively, and to make my requests more clearly. As *Tío* Bill would say, I was communicating EFFECTIVELY.

Until recently, I wasn't very good at the whole "public speaking" thing.

For example, the last time Mrs. Lee made me read in front of the class, she asked me to slow down and breathe deeply. I would always think to myself, what does my breathing have to do with anything?

Well, sometimes I take a while to learn something. I finally understood what she meant.

I concentrated on each of the words I would say. Why rush when I had the chance to be the center of attention? After what I had learned, it was easy for me to talk to the school principal, especially because I already had the permit for the stand. I filed a request to re-open my little stand, using all the phrases necessary for an effective request.

"Principal Lara," I said, armed with the conviction that I was doing something good, "would it be alright if I open my food stand again?"

I wasn't sure I was making a request or an offer. *Tío* Bill says they're different. I don't understand everything he says yet, but you know what? It doesn't matter. I'm taking the initiative and that's what counts.

Principal Lara REQUESTED the menu ahead of time, as well as a picture of what my new stand would look like (Good job Javi! I identified a REQUEST). I've learned that we have to follow certain hygiene rules that the principal has to enforce. Oops, I needed a bigger stand!

"I'll bring you everything in one week," I told her, shortening my own deadlines. "I'll see you then."

Not yet knowing how I was going to get a new stand, I decided to work on the menu first. It was time to work as a

you have to be
prepared for what
others may want
LEARN TO
NEGOTIATE!

team, so I held my first OFFICIAL team meeting with *papi* and Natsuki.

I knew things weren't going to go smoothly at first.

"I think we have to look at grandma's recipe cookbook," said *papi*.

"What if we give the food Japanese names?," added Natsuki.

Fortunately for me, Bill, my uncle, had warned me about the possibility of a FIASCO. He lent me a book called "Conversations for Action," and I learned "new practices for having team conversations"—ways to discuss ideas while building teamwork.

I made sure we kept our spirits up during our first meeting, handing out sweet, sugary cupcakes.

To reach the whole neighbourhood, I had to make an OFFER, and of course an offer wasn't just the product. I had already learned that we're talking about a whole experience.

We needed to make a DESIGN for the stand itself, the food and the service we were delivering. I had to think about the opportunity space, something Tio Bill tried to explain, but I

127

never understood what that really meant before.

Tio Bill had suggested that I think about those areas like regions on a map, a map of people's choices. Where on the map was there an opportunity for my little food stand?

Papi was still struggling a bit to keep up with these new ideas. It wasn't easy to just warm up to them overnight.

"*Papi*," I said, resting one hand on his shoulder, "changing the recipe isn't a sin, and besides, it's for a good cause."

I reminded him how much he likes to cook. Our only choice was to go back to the kitchen and really dare to use other ingredients.

After a round of experimentation, we focused on a new product line: *empanadas* with tofu and ginger, *empanadas* that were like a gyoza with sukyaki sauce, short ribs *empanadas*, along with the two traditional *empanadas* that my dad loved so much.

give people access to hearty
≡MeAL-LiKe≡ snack foods that
didn't feel like JUNK food.

OppORTuniTy

With FUSION
new flavors!

in a ≡modern≡
yet FUN ≡KiDLiKe≡
way.

We left the Spanish *tortilla*, which was one of the kids' favorites, but we also made a vegetable version for adults who were concerned about carbohydrates.

Papi was describing his recipe for Spanish *tortilla* using a particular, "yellower" potato that we couldn't find at out local market. Another Javi mission: find the perfect potato. I called

Define your area of OPPORTUNITY!!!

many markets, finding nothing until I finally discovered this farm about 100 miles from here. They wouldn't deliver them to us because our order was too small.

So I had to do even MORE talking, and get the local supermarket to order it. Boy did I practice all kinds of ways of making a request. Every time I was told "no", I changed something in how I wanted the potatoes and finally, by when I needed them. I realized I could be flexible. It did not hurt that my baby sister Amalia came with me to the supermarket to speak with the store buyers---people find everything SHE does irresistible

"Look," the manager told me, "I'll give you the normal price for potatoes, but I can't give you the merchant wholesale price."

Then my sister and I used our "puss'n'boots" eyes. The manager realized we were negotiating, but for some reason he couldn't resist the charm of the Vega sisters and he gave us the wholesale price.

After working on Saturday, I had to release a lot of steam on Sunday. So I laced up my old tennis shoes, grabbed my racket and went to practice against the back wall. It felt good to get some exercise, but something wasn't completely right.

I went looking for my favorite contender: Aaron Scott.

"Are you challenging me, Javi?," he said, very sure of himself. "You know that I'm a much better tennis player than you."

Now that I think about it, he's the only one who knew that I actually played tennis.

"We'll see."

We went to the neighbourhood tennis court together. We played for over an hour and a half. Aaron was no longer the same cry baby, he was much stronger and faster. Now he was a fantastic rival. It was like playing against a little cannon.

Actually, tennis was a lot of fun. But maybe I didn't need to be the best tennis player in the universe. Did I want to go to tennis camp because the *Comadres* were going there that summer?

I don't think being part of that group was really that important, but I think they represented something I really WAS looking for: EXCELLENCE. I thought that taking lots of classes was the way to go. But the reality of our family budget had become clearer to me through this whole food stand experience. Mom and Dad work so hard, they're still trying to help our family get ahead. For now, expensive classes aren't part of the budget.

Running, on the other hand, is different. I always run, at least when I'm not talking or don't have my head in the clouds.

Maybe I can make running MY sport. The food stand has taught me that excelling at and committing to something is more important than taking very expensive classes. Running is a much cheaper sport than tennis camp. And I love running with a passion. Still, I had to train hard if I wanted to run marathons.

Anyway, there are less than three weeks until the camp, and I don't think I'll be able to raise the money in time for that. The thought of not having to re-launch the food stand in a hurry put a smile on my face. I could prepare my stand with DEDICATION, not in a rush like I did the first time.

To my great surprise, many teachers, parents and a few students had been asking about the little stand. Even though we'd not been open very long, people thought we were just going to be there forever. I was worried about Mrs. Lee, because she had gone back to those ugly sandwiches with white bread, bologna and mayonnaise. That couldn't be good for anyone, much less for a person who worked all day with loud, talkative children.

If you want to make GREAT things happen achieve excellence COMMIT to what you love!

Then it came to me. A REVELATION: My little stand wasn't just an offer anymore, it was a NECESSITY. I had to hurry, so I made a draft menu following my *Tío* Bill's instructions. I printed what's called a "dummy" of the menu. When *Tío* Bill first suggested that I do a "dummy," well, you can imagine what I was thinking!

Tio Bill said the dummy would give me INSIGHTS into what we needed to changed based on what people told us.

So, I had to test my idea before spending money on anything. That would help save money, energy and everything that goes into the final product. The dummy would give me insights as to what we need to change based on people's opinions.

TESTING, TESTING, TESTING

And it didn't just provide valuable information on the menu options. Several teachers took the initiative to print more copies and asked students for their opinions. It turns out we had to expand our drink options beyond water. People liked fruit, eating healthy, yet they also craved sweets, so I learned that I also had to OFFER a variety of natural fruit smoothies. I was finally getting what this whole OFFER thing was about.

The food stand had become so important to others in the community that I was also able to get them to help: several teachers and students stayed after school for a week to help improve the stand. Natsuki helped me make a drawing of the type of stand we had in mind. It had to look modern, and it would also be covered in metallic aluminium.

Natsuki created a great work of art and a nice logo. Now everybody knew who Natsuki Tanaka was and what she was capable of. Kelly Lopez and her *Comadres* wanted to include their art on the stand, but they all agreed that Natsuki was the most talented among them. Other kids started asking for her drawings. Natsuki was a drawing star, she was finally getting noticed!

So many things had happened that I had forgotten to decide
on a name.

"How can we talk about something that doesn't have a
name?," asked my *papi*. "How can people recommend it to their
neighbours if it's just a little stand with no name?"

Mami and *papi* helped me brainstorm some ideas for the
name. After all, they were the investors (an elegant word that
I learned, which means those who put up the money to get
things started).

The list of ingredients had grown, so the initial amount of
money to set up the stand had also increased. *Tío* Bill helped—

136

he said it was a "safe" investment. The thing is, everyone was talking about my little stand. Even though my family was investing in it, it didn't feel right to use Vega for the stand's name.

Natsuki had played an important role, and I wanted all those who had participated in re-launching my stand to feel like it was their own.

We called it JollyFood Stand.

Natskuki and I made flyers to PROMOTE the stand beyond school premises. We gave them to all the teachers, who in turn passed them out to the students, who handed them out to their neighbors. A virtuous circle.

The JollyFood stand turned out much better than what Natsuki and I had imagined on paper. The stand was modern, but full of color. It became a place for neighbors to gather, to INTERACT (or *CONVIVIR*, which is the word we use in Spanish).

I couldn't take care of the stand all the time. With all my schoolwork and athletics, *mami* and *papi* became more and more involved with the stand. My mom organized her class schedule so she could tend to the stand two days a week. *Papi* started to believe in the stand, so much so that he worked on the weekends so we could keep it open every day. He even thought about opening a second stand near his workplace and —who knows— maybe now he could concentrate on his passion.

I finally had a real offer, like Benji's. Other people, including ADULTS, had helped me accomplish what I had wanted to do.

I had started something that created REAL value for others. Maybe I wasn't going to be a professional tennis player right away. But my persistence and commitment had ultimately led to something very valuable after all.

And who knows. Maybe training to become a star runner is in my future.

When you fall **HARD**, get up and go again. You never know where your adventure is **TAKING** you in the quest for OPPORTUNITY!

From: javiera.vega2001@gmail.com

To : ClaudioMoraV@hotmail.com

Subject: Opportunity Manual Finally!!!

Dear Claudio,

I wanted to thank you for all your help with the carritos.
Papi is finally doing what he loves and I learned how to make opportunity happen.

I did not forget about my promise to you. I took notes along the journey. I finally want to share with you my notes and my thoughts now, looking back on it all. Each note is a lesson I learned along the way.

Looking back on it now, I think there are four different types of lessons I learned:

1.Lessons that have to do with the best or most effective way of asking for something.

2.Lessons that have to with offering something.
3.Lessons that have to with listening.
4.Lessons that have to do with overcoming hurdles.
I will attach my manual here with my thoughts about the lessons mean now.
I hope this is of help for your opportunity adventures to come!
Un abrazo,

Javi.

ATTATCHMENT: javisopportunitymanual.doc

Opportunity Manual

BY
JAVI

Lessons around the most effective way to ask for something.

Lesson

What it means

---

1. Screaming off the top of your lungs only works for a gifted few. Try this strategy at your own risk.

Just saying something out loud in thin air does not mean anyone is listening to you.

And screaming might get people's attention, but it is not the most mature way of expressing what we are asking for

---

2. Unless you are under 6 years old, NO ONE can read your mind. Silence is your biggest enemy!

Unless we express or say what we are asking, it is difficult for most people to read our mind.

Our loving parents or caretakers will make every attempt to guess when we are small children, but this does work for very long.

Lesson

What it means

3. Ask for what
you want. If you
can find a way
to get others
to help, you've
struck gold!

If we want to go after an opportunity, we need other people to help us make things happen in the process. We depend on others for what we are trying to accomplish.

The most common way we do this is by making REQUESTS of others.

4. If you want
to get help, make
a REQUEST using
ACTION phrases not
lazy, whiny, or
demanding bully-
like phrases!

Speaking passively with phrases such as "I wish, it would be great if" or whining about what you are requesting to other people is not the most effective way of making your request.

Use the active form of language instead where you identify clearly what you are requesting and to whom.

Lesson	*What it means*

5. When you ask for something or for help—a RE-QUEST—don't forget to say when and how.

We must be specific about how we want something and by when we are asking for it to happen.

6. Conversation open up new paths for making oportunities happen. Being told no is not the end of the world! There are other conversational moves.

Once you open up a conversation, you have let others know your concern. The conversation is now ongoing.

149

What it means

7. We need to communicate to people why something is important to us, why we are asking for their help.

It is not always obvious to others why we are asking for something. Be prepared to provide context.

8. Be prepared to negotiate.

When someone cannot perform what you are asking in the way we want it, it is always possible to "counter" and change our request or to propose something new.

Lessons that have to do with making an offer.

Lesson	What it means
9. Making opportunity happen is not just about asking for things. We must consider what we are OFFERING.	Offers are another way to communicate with others to make something happen.
10. Opportunities open when we offer value to others.	Offers must be of VALUE to others, this means others must appreciate what we are offering.
11. Offering something is a commitment. To make opportunity happen, we have to follow through with our promise.	An offer is a kind of "promise". We have commited to providing something to someone and that is why we must follow through.

151

| Lesson | What it means |

---

12. Dedicate your-
self with all se-
riousness when ex-
ecuting your offer.
Your offer must be
different.

Every detail counts Put work into making sure your offer stands out.

---

13. Putting
a price on
something involves
calculating
your costs and
understanding
how much value
people place
on your offer.
The difference
is called your
"margin"—now you
are making money.

Don't be afraid to charge money for something that others value. If people value your offer, they will be happy to pay a reasonable price.

What it means

---

14. An offer includes the whole experience.

An offer is not just the thing you are offering. It includes the way you offer it, the place, the look, the feel, the way people feel when they try your offer.

---

15. Get people to talk about your offer.

When people talk about it, it becomes part of their lives, and this is the best way to get others to know about it.

---

16. Define your Area of Opportunity.

Understand the other choices people have for doing the same thing and locate where your offer fits in that space of choices.

17. Make your offers with care.

This one speaks for itself. Take pride in every detail.

18. Commit to what you love to do.

Sometimes our best offers are the things we love to do.

Lessons that have to do with listening.

Lesson	*What it means*
19. Have empathy towards others and show them you are interested in how they feel.	*Empathy involves being attuned or alert to how those around you feel, and letting them know you are paying attention.*
20. QUESTION, QUESTION, AND QUESTION. Opportunities appear when we question what seems obvious.	*Never take knowing something for granted. There is a lot to learn if you dig deep.*
21. OBSERVE and LISTEN to people beyond what they say. When in doubt, ask and listen.	*People don't always know how to express what they want, or if they are not happy with something about your offer. Pay attention to what they don't do and don't say as well.*

155

Lessons that have to do with overcoming hurdles.

Lesson

What it means

22. Don't assume something will not work. Opportunities happen only if we MAKE them happen!	It is easy to lose patience and jump to conclude that something is not working out. We must persist and move forward if we believe in what we are doing.
23. The great opportunity makers fail before having success. Get ready to jump over hurdles.	Making mistakes or failing at something does not mean that we won't succeed in the end. Failing is part of the learning process.

24. Making something happen means teamwork. And teamwork sometimes involves making and receiving "assessments", even if you feel bad about it.

Assessments are nothing more than people's opinion, opinions we can "ground" or provide evidence for or not. They are not facts that reveal something deeply true about us. So we should not take these personally.

25. When you fall hard get up and go again. You never know where your adventure is taking you. This is the quest for opportunity.

Opportunity making is a fun adventure in the end!

Made in the USA
Charleston, SC
10 February 2017